Freemason Burial Services with General Instructions

By ROBERT MACOY

ISBN:978-1-63923-152-2

Masonic Burial Services

with General Instructions

Printed: November 2021

Cover Art By: Paul Amid

Published and Distributed By:

Lushena Books
607 Country Club Drive, Unit E
Bensenville, IL 60106
www.lushenabks.com

ISBN: 978-1-63923-152-2

Printed in the United States of America

The services herein arranged for the Burial of the Dead are adapted for all the purposes for which ceremonies of that character may be required. The arrangement is such that any portion of the service—each part being complete—may be used as occasion requires. It is not expected that the whole ceremony will or can be used at any one time. If the weather should be stormy, or the body of the deceased taken, for interment, to a distance, where it would be impossible for the brethren to attend, that portion of the service set apart for the Lodge-room, or at the house of the deceased, may be performed.

MASONIC FUNERAL SERVICES:

PREPARED BY

ROBERT MACOY,

AUTHOR OF THE MASONIC MANUAL, BOOK OF THE LODGE,
TRUE MASONIC GUIDE, PAST DEPUTY GRAND MASTER,
GRAND RECORDER, ETC.

———————— ›‹ ————————

The Ceremonies which are observed on the occasion of funerals are highly appropriate; they are performed as a melancholy Masonic Duty, and as a token of respect and affection to the memory of a departed brother.

GENERAL DIRECTIONS.

I. No Freemason can be buried with the formalities of the Fraternity, unless it be at his own request, or that of some of his family, communicated to the Master of the Lodge of which he died a member; foreigners or sojourners excepted; nor unless he has received the Master Mason's degree, and from this restriction there can be no exception.

II. Fellow Crafts or Entered Apprentices are not entitled to these obsequies; nor can they be allowed to unite, as Masons, in the funeral of a brother.

III. No Lodge, or body of Masons, can unite in the obsequies of a person not a Mason, without permission of the Grand Master, or consent of the Grand Lodge.

IV. The Master of the Lodge, having received notice of the death of a brother, (the deceased having attained to the degree of Master Mason,) and of his request to be buried with

3

the ceremonies of the Craft, fixes the day and hour for the funeral, (unless previously arranged by the friends or relatives of the deceased,) and issues his command to the Secretary to summon the Lodge. He may invite as many Lodges as he may think proper, and the members of those may accompany their officers in form; but the whole ceremony must be under the direction of the Master of the Lodge of which the deceased was a member.

V. Upon the death of a sojourner, who had expressed a wish to be buried with the Masonic ceremonies, the duties prescribed in Article IV. will devolve upon the Master of the Lodge within whose jurisdiction the death may occur; and if in a place where there be more than one Lodge, then upon the Master of the oldest Lodge, unless otherwise mutually arranged.

VI. Whenever civic societies, or the military, may unite with Masons in the burial of a Mason, the body of the deceased must be in charge of the Lodge having jurisdiction. The Masonic services should in all respects be conducted as if none but Masons were in attendance.

VII. If the deceased was a Grand or Past Grand officer, the officers of the Grand Lodge should be invited; when the Master of the Lodge having jurisdiction, will invite the Grand officer present who has attained the highest rank to conduct the burial service.

VIII. The pall-bearers should be Masons, selected by the Master. If the deceased was a member of a Chapter, Commandery, or Consistory, a portion of the pall-bearers should be taken from these bodies severally.

4

IX. The proper clothing for a Masonic funeral is a black hat, black or dark clothes, black neck-tie, white gloves, and a plain square white linen or lambskin apron, with a band of black crape around the left arm, above the elbow, and a sprig of evergreen on the left breast. The Master's gavel, the Wardens' columns, the Deacons' and Stewards' rods, the Tiler's sword, the Bible, the Book of Constitutions, and the Marshal's baton, should be trimmed with black crape, neatly tied with white ribbon. The officers of the Lodge should, and Past Masters and Grand Officers may, wear their official jewels.

X. While the body is lying in the coffin, there should be placed upon the latter a plain white lambskin apron.

XI. If a Past or Present Grand Master, Deputy Grand Master, or Grand Warden, should join the procession of a private Lodge, proper attention must be paid to them. They take place after the Master of the Lodge. Two Deacons, with white rods, should be appointed by the Master to attend a Grand Warden; and when the Grand Master or Deputy Grand Master is present, the Book of Constitutions should be borne before him, a Sword-Bearer should follow, and the Deacons, with white rods, on his right and left.

XII. When the head of the procession shall have arrived at the place of interment, or where the services are to be performed, the lines should be opened, and the highest officer in rank, preceded by the Marshal and Tiler pass through, and the others follow in order.

XIII. Upon arriving at the entrance of the cemetery, the brethren should march in open order to the tomb or grave. If the body is to be placed in the former, the Tiler should

5

take his place in front of the open door, and the lines be spread so as to form a circle. The coffin should be deposited in the circle, and the Stewards and Deacons should cross their rods over it. The bearers should take their places on either side—the mourners at the foot of the coffin, and the Master and other officers at the head. After the coffin has been placed in the tomb, the Stewards should cross their rods over the door, and the Deacons over the Master.—If the body is to be deposited in the earth, the circle should be formed around the grave, the body being placed on rests over it; the Stewards should cross their rods over the foot, and the Deacons the head, and retain their places throughout the services.

XIV. After the clergymen shall have performed the religious services of the Church, the Masonic services should begin.

XV. When a number of Lodges join in a funeral procession, the position of the youngest Lodge is at the head or right of the procession, and the oldest at the end or left, excepting that the Lodge of which deceased was a member walks nearest the corpse.

XVI. The procession must return to the Lodge-room in the same order in which it marched to the grave.

XVII. A Lodge in procession is to be strictly under the discipline of the Lodge-room, therefore, no brother can enter the procession or leave it without express permission from the Master, conveyed through the Marshal.

6

SERVICE

IN THE

LODGE-ROOM

The brethren having assembled at the Lodge-room, the Lodge will be opened briefly in the third degree; the purpose of the communication must be stated; and remarks upon the character of the deceased may be made by the Master and brethren, when the service will commence—all the brethren to stand:

Master. What man is he that liveth, and shall not see death? Shall he deliver his soul from the hand of the grave?

Sen. War. His days are as grass; as a flower of the field, so he flourisheth.

Jun. War. For the wind passeth over it, and it is gone; and the place thereof shall know it no more.

Master. Where is now our departed Brother?

Sen. War. He dwelleth in night; he sojourneth in darkness.

Jun. War. Man walketh in a vain shadow; he heapeth up riches, and cannot tell who shall gather them.

Master. When he dieth, he shall carry nothing away; his glory shall not descend after him.

7

Sen. War. For he brought nothing into the world and it is certain he can carry nothing out.

Jun. War. The LORD gave, and the LORD hath taken away; blessed be the name of the LORD.

Master. The LORD is merciful and gracious, slow to anger, and plenteous in mercy.

Sen. War. GOD is our salvation; our glory, and the rock of our strength; and our refuge is in GOD.

Jun. War. He hath not dealt with us after our sins, nor rewarded us according to our iniquities.

Master. Can we offer any precious gift acceptable in the sight of the LORD to redeem our brother?

Sen. War. We are poor and needy. We are without gift or ransom.

Jun. War. Be merciful unto us, O LORD, be merciful unto us; for we trust in thee. Our hope and salvation are in thy patience. Where else can we look for mercy?

Master. Let us endeavor to live the life of the righteous, that our last end may be like his.

Sen. War. The LORD is gracious and righteous; yea, our GOD is merciful.

8

Jun. War. GOD is our GOD for ever and ever. He will be our guide, even unto death.

Master. Shall our brother's name and virtues be lost upon the earth forever?

Response by the Brethren. We will remember and cherish them in our hearts.

Master. I heard a voice from heaven, saying unto me, "Write, from henceforth blessed are the dead who die in the LORD! Even so, saith the Spirit; for they rest from their labors."

Here the Master will take the SACRED ROLL,* on which have been inscribed the name, age date of initiation or affiliation, date of death, and any matters that may be interesting to the brethren; and shall read the same aloud, and shall then say,

ALMIGHTY FATHER! in tny hands we leave, with humble submission, the soul of our departed brother.

Response. Amen! So mote it be!

The grand honors† should then be given three times; the brethren to respond each time—

The will of GOD is accomplished.—AMEN! So mote it be!

* A sheet of parchment or paper, prepared for the purpose.
† See note, p. 336

The Master should then deposit the ROLL, in the archives of the Lodge,

The following or some other appropriate HYMN may be sung :

AIR—BALERMA. C. M.

Few are thy days, and full of woe, O

man, of wo-man born! Thy doom is writ-ten

"Dust thou art, And shalt to dust re-turn."

Behold the emblem of thy state
In flowers that bloom and die ;
Or in the shadows fleeting form,
That mocks the gazer's eye.

Determined are the days that fly
Successive o'er thy head ;
The number'd hour is on the wing,
That lays thee with the dead.

Great GOD, afflict not, in thy wrath,
The short alloted span
That bounds the few and weary days
Of pilgrimage to man.

The Master or Chaplain will repeat the following or some other appropriate PRAYER:

ALMIGHTY AND HEAVENLY FATHER—infinite in wisdom, mercy, and goodness—extend to us the riches of thy everlasting grace. Thou alone art a refuge and help in trouble and affliction. In this bereavement we look to thee for support and consolation. May we believe that death hath no power over a faithful and righteous soul! May we believe that, though the dust returneth to the dust as it was, the spirit goeth unto thyself. As we mourn the departure of a brother beloved from the circle of our Fraternity, may we trust that he hath entered into a higher brotherhood, to engage in nobler duties and in

14*

heavenly work, to find rest from earthly labor, and refreshment from earthly care. May thy peace abide within us, to keep us from all evil! Make us grateful for present benefits, and crown us with immortal life and honor.— And to thy name shall be all the glory for-ever.—AMEN.

Response. So mote it be.

A procession should then be formed, which will proceed to the church or the house of the deceased, in the following order:

Tiler, with drawn sword;
Stewards, with white rods;
Master Masons;
Secretary and Treasurer;
Senior and Junior Wardens;
Past Masters;
The Holy Bible,

On a cushion, covered with black cloth, carried by the oldest member of the Lodge.

THE MASTER,

Supported by two Deacons, with white rods.

When the head of the procession arrives at the entrance of the building, it should halt and open to the right and left, forming two parallel lines, when the Marshal, with the Tiler, will pass through the lines to end, and escort the Master or Grand Officer into the house, the brethren closing in and following, thus reversing the order of procession—the breth ren with heads uncovered.

12

SERVICE

CHURCH OR THE HOUSE OF THE DECEASED.

After the religious services have been performed, the
Master will take his station at the head of the coffin, the
Senior Warden on his right, the Junior Warden on his left;
the Deacons and Stewards, with white rods crossed, the former
at the head and the latter at the foot of the coffin; the brethren
forming a circle around all, when the Masonic service will
commence by the Chaplain or Master repeating the following
or some other appropriate PRAYER, in which all the brethren
will join.

Our Father which art in heaven, hallowed
be thy name. Thy kingdom come. Thy will
be done in earth as it is in heaven. Give us
this day our daily bread. And forgive us our
debts, as we forgive our debtors. And lead us
not into temptation, but deliver us from evil.
For thine is the kingdom, and the power, and
the glory, for ever.—AMEN.

Master. Brethren, we are called upon by
the imperious mandate of the dread messenger
Death, against whose free entrance within the
circle of our Fraternity the barred doors and
Tiler's weapon offer no impediment, to mourn

the loss of one of our companions. The dead body of our beloved Brother A . . . . B . . . . lies in its narrow house before us, overtaken by that fate which must sooner or later overtake us all; and which no power or station, no virtue or bravery, no wealth or honor, no tears of friends or agonies of relatives can avert; teaching an impressive lesson, continually repeated, yet soon forgotten, that every one of us must ere long pass through the valley of the shadow of death, and dwell in the house of darkness.

Sen. War. In the midst of life we are in death; of whom may we seek for succor but of thee, O LORD, who for our sins art justly displeased. Thou knowest, LORD, the secrets of our hearts; shut not thy merciful ears to our prayer.

Jun. War. LORD, let me know my end, and the number of my days; that I may be certified how long I have to live.

Master. Man that is born of women is of few days and full of trouble. He cometh forth as a flower, and is cut down; he fleeth also as a shadow, and continueth not. Seeing his days are determined, the number of his months are

14

with thee, thou hast appointed his bounds that he cannot pass; turn from him that he may rest, till he shall accomplish his day. For there is hope of a tree, if it be cut down, that it will sprout again, and that the tender branch thereof will not cease. But man dieth and wasteth away; yea, man giveth up the ghost, and where is he? As the waters fail from the sea, and the flood decayeth and drieth up, so man lieth down, and riseth not up till the heavens shall be no more.

Sen. War. Our life is but a span long, and the days of our pilgrimage are few and full of evil.

Jun. War. So teach us to number our days, that we may apply our hearts unto wisdom.

Master. Man goeth forth to his work and to his labor until the evening of his day. The labor and work of our brother are finished. As it hath pleased ALMIGHTY GOD to take the soul of our departed brother, may he find mercy in the great day when all men shall be judged according to the deeds done in the body. We must walk in the light while we have light; for the darkness of death may come upon us, at a time when we may not be prepared. Take

15

heed, therefore, watch and pray; for ye know not when the time is; ye know not when the Master cometh, at even; at midnight,or in the morning. We should so regulate our lives by the line of rectitude and truth, that in the evening of our days we may be found worthy to be called from labor to refreshment, and duly prepared for a translation from the terrestrial to the celestial Lodge, to join the Fraternity of the spirits of just men made perfect.

Sen. War. Behold, O LORD, we are in distress! Our hearts are turned within us; there is none to comfort us; our sky is darkened with clouds, and mourning and lamentations are heard among us.

Jun. War. Our life is a vapor that appeareth for a little while, and then vanisheth away. All flesh is as grass, and all the glory of man as the flower of grass. The grass withereth, and the flower thereof falleth away.

Master. It is better to go to the house of mourning than to go to the house of feasting; for that is the end of all men; and the living will lay it to his heart.

Response by all the Brethren. So mote it be.

16

Then may be sung the following or some other appropriate
HYMN :

NAOMI. C. M. Dr. L. Mason.

1st Tenor
2d Tenor

Here Death his sa - cred seal hath set, On

2d Bass
1st Bass

Bright and by-gone hours ; The dead we mourn are

with us yet, And—more than ev - er— ours!

Ours, by the pledge of love and faith ;
  By hopes of heaven on high ;
By trust, triumphant over death,
  In immortality !

The dead are like the stars by day,
  Withdrawn from mortal eye ;
Yet holding unperceived their way
  Through the unclouded sky.

17

By them, through holy hope and love,
We feel, in hours serene,
Connected with the Lodge above,
Immortal and unseen,

The MASTER or CHAPLAIN will repeat the following or some other appropriate PRAYER:

MOST GLORIOUS GOD! author of all good, and giver of all mercy! pour down thy blessings upon us, and strengthen our solemn engagements with the ties of sincere affection! May the present instance of mortality remind us of our approaching fate, and draw our attention toward thee, the only refuge in time of need! that when the awful moment shall arrive, that we are about to quit this transitory scene, the enlivening prospect of thy mercy may dispel the gloom of death; and after our departure hence in peace and in thy favor, we may be received into thine everlasting kingdom, to enjoy, in union with the souls of our departed friends, the just reward of a pious and virtuous life.

Response. So mote it be.

If the remains of the deceased are to be removed to a distance where the brethren cannot follow to perform the ceremonies at the grave, the procession will return to the Lodge-room or disperse, as most convenient.

18

SERVICE AT THE GRAVE.

When the solemn rites of the dead are to be performed at the grave, the procession should be formed, and proceed to the place of interment in the following order:

Tiler, with drawn sword;
Stewards, with white rods;
Musicians,
If they are Masons, otherwise they follow the Tiler;
Master Masons;
Secretary and Treasurer;
Senior and Junior Wardens;
Past Masters;
The Holy Writings,
On a cushion, covered with black cloth, carried by the oldest member of the Lodge.
THE MASTER,
Supported by two Deacons, with white rods;
Officiating Clergy;

MARSHAL.

The
with the insignia
Pall-bearers;

Body,
placed thereon;
Pall-bearers;

Mourners.

If the deceased was a member of a Royal Arch Chapter and a Commandery of Knights Templar, and members of those bodies should unite in the procession, clothed as such, the former will follow the Past Masters, and the latter will act as an escort or guard of honor to the corpse, outside the Pall bearers, marching in the form of a triangle; the officers

19

of the Commandery forming the base of the triangle, with the Eminent Commander in the center.

When the procession has arrived at the place of interment, the members of the Lodge should form a circle around the grave; when the Master, Chaplain, and other Officers of the acting Lodge, take their position at the head of the grave, and the mourners at the foot.

After the Clergyman has performed the religious service of the Church, the Masonic service should begin.

THE Chaplain rehearses the following or some other appropriate PRAYER.

ALMIGHTY and most merciful Father, we adore thee as the God of time and eternity. As it has pleased thee to take from the light of our abode one dear to our hearts, we beseech thee to bless and sanctify unto us this dispensation of thy providence. Inspire our hearts with wisdom from on high, that we may glorify thee in all our ways. May we realize that thine all-seeing eye is upon us

20

and be influenced by the spirit of truth and love to perfect obedience—that we may enjoy the divine approbation here below. And when our toils on earth shall have ended, may we be raised to the enjoyment of fadeless light and immortal life in that kingdom where faith and hope shall end—and love and joy prevail through eternal ages. And thine, O righteous Father, shall be the glory forever.—AMEN.

Response.—So mote it be.

The following exhortation is then given by the Master:

BRETHREN: The solemn notes that betoken the dissolution of this earthly tabernacle, have again alarmed our outer door, and another spirit has been summoned to the land where our fathers have gone before us. Again we are called to assemble among the habitations of the dead, to behold the "narrow house appointed for all living." Here, around us, in that peace which the world cannot give or take away, sleep the unnumbered dead. The gentle breeze fans their verdant covering, they it heed not; the sunshine and the storm pass over them, and they are not disturbed; stones and lettered monuments symbolize the affection of surviving friends, yet no sound proceeds from them, save that silent but thrilling admonition, "Seek ye the narrow path and the straight gate that lead unto eternal life."

We are again called upon to consider the uncertainty of human life; the immutable certainty of death, and the vanity of all human pursuits. Decrepitude and decay are written upon every living thing. The cradle and the coffin stand in juxtaposition to each other; and it is a melancholy truth, that so soon as we begin to live, that moment also we begin to die. It is passing strange that, notwithstanding the daily mementos of mortality that cross our path; notwithstanding the funeral bell so often tolls in our ears, and the "mournful procession" go about our streets, that we will not more seriously consider our approaching fate. We go on from design to design, add hope to hope, and lay out plans for the employment of many years, until we are suddenly alarmed at the approach of the Messenger of Death, at a moment when we least expect him, and which we probably conclude to be the meridian of our existence.

What, then, are all the externals of human dignity, the power of wealth, the dreams of

22

ambition, the pride of intellect, or the charms of beauty, when Nature has paid her just debt? Fix your eyes on the last sad scene, and view life stript of its ornaments, and exposed in its natural meanness, and you must be persuaded of the utter emptiness of these delusions. In the grave, all fallacies are detected, all ranks are leveled, all distinctions are done away. Here the sceptre of the prince and the staff of the beggar are laid side by side.

While we drop the sympathetic tear over the grave of our deceased brother, let us cast around his foibles, whatever they may have been, the *broad mantle of Masonic charity*, nor withhold from his memory the commendation that his virtues claim at our hands. Perfection on earth has never yet been attained; the wisest, as well as the best of men, have gone astray. Suffer, then, the apologies of human nature to plead for him who can no longer plead for himself.

Our present meeting and proceedings will have been vain and useless, if they fail to excite our serious reflections, and strengthen our resolutions of amendment. Be then persuaded, my brethren, by this example, of the uncertainty of human life—of the unsubstan-

23

tial nature of all its pursuits, and no longer
postpone the all-important concern of prepar-
ing for eternity. Let us each embrace the
present moment, and while time and oppor-
tunity permit, prepare with care for that great
change which we all know must come, when
the pleasures of the world shall cease to de-
light, and be as a poison to our lips; and
while we may enjoy the happy reflection of a
well-spent life in the exercise of piety and
virtue, will yield the only comfort and consolation. Thus shall our hopes be not frus-
trated, nor we hurried unprepared into the
presence of that all-wise and powerful Judge,
to whom the secrets of all hearts are known.
Let us resolve to maintain with sincerity the
dignified character of our profession. May
our *faith* be evinced in a correct moral walk
and deportment; may our *hope* be bright as
the glorious mysteries that will be revealed
hereafter; and our *charity* boundless as the
wants of our fellow-creatures. And having
faithfully discharged the great duties which
we owe to GOD, to our neighbor, and our-
selves; when at last it shall please the Grand
Master of the universe to summon us into his
eternal presence, may the *trestle-board* of our

SERVICE AT THE GRAVE.

whole lives pass such inspection that it may
be given unto each of us to "eat of the hidden
manna," and to receive the "white stone with
a new name" that will insure perpetual and
unspeakable happiness at his right hand.

The Master then, (presenting the apron) continues:

The lambskin or white apron, is the emblem
of innocence and the badge of a Mason.   It
is more ancient than the Golden Fleece or
Roman Eagle; more honorable than the Star
and Garter when worthily worn.

The Master then deposits it in the grave.

This emblem I now deposit in the grave of
our deceased brother.   By it we are reminded
of the universal dominion of Death.   The arm
of Friendship cannot interpose to prevent his
coming; the wealth of the world cannot pur-
chase our release; nor will the innocence of
youth, or the charms of beauty propitiate his
purpose.   The mattock, the coffin, and the
melancholy grave, admonish us of our mortality, and that, sooner or later, these frail bodies
must moulder in their parent dust.

The Master (holding the evergreen) continues:

25

This *evergreen*, which once marked the temporary resting-place of the illustrious dead, is an emblem of our faith in the immortality of the soul. By this we are reminded that we have an immortal part within us, that shall survive the grave, and which shall never, *never*, NEVER, die. By it we are admonished that, though, like our brother, whose remains lie before us, we shall soon be clothed in the habiliments of DEATH, and deposited in the silent tomb, yet, through our belief in the mercy of GOD, we may confidently hope that our souls will bloom in eternal spring. This, too, I deposit in the grave, with the exclamation, "Alas, my brother!"

The Brethren then move in procession around the place of interment, and severally drop the sprig of evergreen into the grave; after which, the public grand honors* are given.

* The grand honors practiced among Masons during the burial ceremonies, either in public or private, are given in the following manner: Both arms are crossed on the breast, the left uppermost, and the open palms of the hands striking the shoulders; they are then raised above the head, the palms striking each other and then made to fall sharply on the thighs, with the head bowed. This is repeated three times. While the honors are being given the third time, the brethren audibly pronounce the following words—when the arms are crossed on the breast:—"We cherish his memory here;" when the hands are extended above the head—"We commend his spirit to GOD who gave it;" and when the hands are extended toward the ground—"And consign his body to the earth."

26

The Master then continues the ceremony:

From time immemorial, it has been the custom among the Fraternity of Free and Accepted Masons, at the request of a brother, to accompany his remains to the place of interment, and there to deposit them with the usual formalities.

In conformity to this usage, and at the request of our deceased brother, whose memory we revere, and whose loss we now deplore, we have assembled in the character of Masons, to offer up to his memory, before the world, the last tribute of our affection; thereby demonstrating the sincerity of our past esteem for him, and our steady attachment to the principles of the Order.

The Great Creator having been pleased, out of his infinite mercy, to remove our brother from the cares and troubles of this transitory existence, to a state of endless duration, thus severing another link from the fraternal chain that binds us together; may we, who survive him, be more strongly cemented in the ties of union and friendship; that, during the short space allotted us here, we may wisely and usefully employ our time; and in the reciprocal intercourse of kind and friendly acts, mutually promote the welfare and happiness of each other. Unto the grave we have consigned the body of our deceased brother; earth to earth (*earth being sprinkled on the coffin*), ashes to ashes, (*more earth*), dust to dust, (*more earth*); there to remain till the trump shall sound on the resurrection morn. We can cheerfully leave him in the hands of a Being, who has done all things well; who is glorious in holiness, fearful in praises, doing wonders.

To those of his immediate relatives and friends, who are most heart-stricken at the loss we have all sustained, we have but little of this world's consolation to offer. We can only sincerely, deeply, and most affectionately sympathize with them in their afflictive bereavement. But we can say, that HE who tempers the wind to the shorn lamb, looks down with infinite compassion upon the widow and fatherless, in the hour of their desolation; and that the Great Architect will fold the arms of his love and protection around those who put their trust in him.

Then let us improve this solemn warning that at last, when the sheeted dead are stirring, when the great white throne is set, we shall receive from the Omniscient Judge, the thrilling invita-

28

tion, Come, ye blessed, inherit the kingdom prepared for you from the foundation of the world.

The following, or some other suitable ODE, may be sung:

SCOTLAND.

Arranged from Dr. CLARK, by Br. JAS. B. TAYLOR.

Thou art gone to the grave, but we will not de -

plore thee, Tho' sor-row and darkness en-compass the

tomb ; The Good has pass'd on thro' its

29

por - tals be - fore thee, And the cas - sia

blooms green-ly to light - en the gloom, And the

cas - sia blooms green-ly to light - en the gloom.

Thou art gone to the grave; we no longer behold thee,
  Nor tread the rough paths of the world by thy hand;
But the wide arms of Mercy are spread to enfold thee,
  And we'll meet thee again in the heavenly land.

Thou art gone to the grave; and its mansion forsaking,
  Perchance thy weak spirit in doubt lingered long;
But the sunshine of heaven beamed bright on thy waking
  And the sound thou didst hear was the seraphim's song.

SERVICE AT THE GRAVE.

Thou art gone to the grave ; but 'twere wrong to deplore
     thee,
  When GOD was thy trust and thy guardian and guide :
He gave thee, He took thee, and soon will restore thee
In the blest Lodge above where the faithful abide.

Or this :

PLEYEL'S HYMN.

Sol - emn strikes the fun - ral chime, Notes of our de-part-ing time; As we jour - ney here be- low. Thro' a pil - grim-age of woe.

Mortals, now indulge a tear,
For Mortality is here!
See how wide her trophies wave
O'er the slumbers of the grave!

Here another guest we bring;
Seraphs of celestial wing,
To our fun'ral altar come,
Waft our friend and brother home.

There, enlarged, thy soul shall see
What was vailed in mystery;
Heavenly glories of the place
Show his Maker face to face.

LORD of all! below—above—
Fill our hearts with truth and love;
When dissolves our earthly tie,
Take us to thy Lodge on high.

The service may be concluded with the following or some other suitable PRAYER:

MOST GLORIOUS GOD, author of all good and giver of all mercy, pour down thy blessings upon us and strengthen our solemn engagements with the ties of sincere affection. May the present instance of mortality remind us of our own approaching fate, and, by drawing our attention toward thee, the only refuge in time of need, may we be induced so to regulate our conduct here, that when the awful moment shall arrive, at which we must quit this transitory scene, the enlivening prospect of thy mercy may dispel the gloom of death; and that after our departure hence in peace and thy favor, we may be received into thine everlasting kingdom, and there join in union with our friend, and enjoy that uninterrupted and unceasing felicity which is allotted to the souls of just men made perfect.— AMEN,

Response.—So mote it be.

Master. The will of GOD is accomplished.

Response. So mote it be.

Master. From dust we came, and unto dust we must return.

Response. May we all be recompensed at the resurrection of the just.—AMEN.

Thus the service ends, and the procession will return in form to the place whence it set out, where the necessary business of Masonry should be renewed. The insignia and ornaments of the deceased, if an officer of a Lodge, are to be returned to the Master, with the usual ceremonies, and the Lodge will be closed in form.

REGULATIONS FOR PROCESSIONS.

When the Grand Master, Deputy Grand Master, or either of the Grand Wardens, joins the procession of a private Lodge, proper respect is to be paid to the rank of that officer. His position will be immediately before the Master and Wardens of the Lodge, and two Deacons will be appointed to attend him.

When the Grand or Deputy Grand Master is present, the Book of Constitutions will be borne before him. The honor of carrying this book belongs of right to the Master of the oldest Lodge in the jurisdiction, whenever he is present. The Book of Constitutions must never be borne in a procession unless the Grand or Deputy Grand Master be present.

In entering public buildings, the Bible, Square and Compasses, and the Book of Constitutions, are to be placed in front of the Grand Master, and the Grand Marshal and Grand Deacons must keep near him.

When a procession faces inward, the Deacons and Stewards will cross their rods, so as to form an arch for the brethren to pass beneath.

Marshals are to walk or ride on the left flank of a procession The appropriate costume of a Marshal is a cocked hat, sword and scarf, with a baton in his hand. The color of the scarf must be blue in the procession of a Subordinate Lodge, and purple in that of the Grand Lodge.

All processions will return in the same order in which they set out.

The post of honor in a Masonic procession is always in the rear.

34

9781639231522